S0-ART-899

# Idina Menzel

Broadway Superstar

**STAGE STARS**

*Volume 2*

**A Children's Biography by**
*Christine Dzidrums*

# Idina Menzel
## Broadway Superstar

**STAGE STARS**
## Volume 2

**A Children's Biography by**
*Christine Dzidrums*

CREATIVE MEDIA, INC.
PO Box 6270
Whittier, California 90609-6270
United States of America

If you purchased this book without a cover, you should be aware that this book is stolen property. It was reported as "unsold and destroyed" to the publisher, and neither the author nor the publisher has received any payment for this "stripped book."

The scanning, uploading, and distribution of this book via the Internet or via any other means without the permission of the publisher is illegal and punishable by law. Please purchase only authorized electronic editions and do not participate in or encourage electronic piracy of copyrighted materials. Your support of the authors' rights is appreciated.

The publisher does not have any control and does not assume any responsibility for author or third-party website or their content.

www.creativemedia.net

Cover and Book design by Joseph Dzidrums
Front cover photo by Anthony G. Moore / PR Photos
Back cover photo by FOX Broadcasting Company

Copyright © 2013 by Creative Media, Inc. All rights reserved.
Printed in the United States of America.

First Edition: March 2013

Library of Congress Control Number: 2013934478

ISBN 978-1-938438-17-2                    10 9 8 7 6 5 4 3 2 1

Thank you, Elizabeth and Leah,
the most amazing sisters ever.

**This book is dedicated to every "Elphaba"
still struggling to find their voice.**

# TABLE OF CONTENTS

*"Fake it until you make it."*

# A BIG TOMORROW
## Chapter One

On May 30, 1971, Stuart and Helen Mentzel, a young married couple living in Queens, welcomed their daughter Idina Kim Mentzel into the world. The proud parents named their first child after her great-grandmother Ida. Three years later, they were blessed with a second girl, Cara Leigh.

As the years passed the family moved to nearby Woodbury. Helene earned a living as a therapist, while Stuart worked as a pajama salesman. The young father's industry connections ensured that his beautiful daughters always wore the most stylish sleep clothes.

"I had the prettiest baby doll outfits," Idina later giggled. "His big clients, Kmart and Target, put me through college."

One summer day five-year-old Idina and her friends sang Harry Chapin's "Cat's in the Cradle" during a music class at camp. Suddenly the youngster grew bored and began harmonizing the folk classic. The counselors gawked at the green-eyed brunette who belted complicated notes with little effort. They'd never seen such talent in all their years of teaching.

Soon Idina's singing flooded the Mentzel home. If anyone happened to walk by the family's house, they might hear the precocious child belting out selections from the musical *Annie*, especially the hopeful anthem "Tomorrow." Stuart and Helen often shook their heads in amazement. How did someone so tiny have such big pipes?

One day Idina discovered that her school was mounting a talent show. The thought of singing for a big crowd excited the outgoing child.

When school let out, the budding performer grabbed a permission slip and sprinted all the way home. By the time she reached her house, the youngster huffed and puffed while clutching her side.

"Mom, can I audition for the talent show?" she gasped between breaths.

A few weeks later Idina walked onto her school's stage for her big solo singing debut. When she peered out into the crowd, nearly a hundred people looked back. Butterflies suddenly invaded her stomach. The youngster took a deep breath and then launched into an impressive rendition of "The Way We Were." Jaws dropped as amazed adults looked at one another in wonder. When the future superstar finished, the audience gave her a standing ovation while she grinned excitedly. Now that was fun!

Idina didn't just love singing, though. She adored listening to other great singers, too. Above all other performers, she liked Barbra Streisand best. The stunning vocalist possessed perfect pitch, crystal clear delivery, an impressive range and interpreted songs like no other. The young fan often wondered how it might feel to sing like Barbra.

In the meantime Idina began saving her weekly allowances to build a music library. For her first album, she purchased the 1976 soundtrack to *A Star is Born*. Featuring songs from the Barbra Streisand and Kris Kristofferson remake, the best seller boasted several hits, including the Oscar-winning "Evergreen."

Although Barbra always remained Idina's favorite singer, she enjoyed Top 40 music, too. Her diverse album collection soon featured artists like Madonna and Whitney Houston.

Meanwhile Idina continued singing all the time. She sang so often that Stuart and Helen worried the prodigy might ruin her voice, so they enrolled her in formal lessons. The adolescent's coach felt the young girl possessed remarkable talent, but she occasionally shouted songs. She would teach her pupil correct vocal techniques.

Happy to encourage their daughter's interest, Idina's parents often organized family trips to Manhattan to watch musicals. The Mentzel girls loved wearing pretty dresses and watching trained actors tell stories through music and dance. The elder sister especially liked *Dreamgirls* and *Annie* and fantasized about one day performing in such shows.

In fifth grade Idina played Dorothy in her school's production of *The Wizard of Oz*. The natural entertainer particularly loved singing the musical's famous ballad "Somewhere Over the Rainbow." A few months later, she played Mabel in Gilbert and Sullivan's comic opera *The Pirates of Penzance*.

Idina continued her acting career years later at Syosset High School, when she auditioned for its production of Rodgers and Hammerstein's *Carousel*. When the cast list was posted, the nervous teen scanned the list for her name. She shook her head in confusion upon learning that the show's director had cast her as Nettie, the maternal figure that sings the inspirational "You'll Never Walk Alone."

**LONG ISLAND WEDDING SINGER**
(Tom Walck/PR Photos)

"Nettie?" a confused Idina repeated. "The oldest woman in the play? Why?"

Syosset High's drama teacher explained that the talented teen owned the school's most mature voice. In the end the performer delivered a surprisingly astute performance that belied her young age. When the dynamo singer took her curtain call, the audience cheered enthusiastically.

Meanwhile Idina experienced a relatively normal teenage life. She formed several lasting friendships, including one with an immensely gifted singer named Adam Pascal, a powerful, handsome rocker.

At just fifteen years old, Idina's life changed forever when her mother and father announced they were divorcing, citing irreconcilable differences. Although their split devastated the high school student, she found comfort through her singing.

Shortly afterward Idina began voice lessons with Mr. Arnold, a classical instructor. The well-rounded teenager soon cultivated an impressive range of musical tastes and emulated powerful, soulful singers, like Aretha Franklin, Etta James, Gladys Knight and Chaka Kahn.

Many parents in the Mentzel's affluent neighborhood gave their spoiled offspring big allowances. The teenagers often spent the money by throwing lavish, alcohol-filled parties. Idina, however, had little interest in mindless partying. She would spend her time productively and earn her own money.

Shunning retail and fast food jobs, Idina interviewed for a local wedding band. The gig required an eighteen-year-old lead singer, so the teen fudged her age by three years and won the job. The versatile vocalist sung many musical styles: jazz, rock, show tunes, and Motown. On weekends the teen with giant '80s hair demonstrated the limbo, played the tambourine or reenacted the electric slide, a popular line dance craze. She also mastered frequently requested wedding songs "The Girl From Ipanema," "Conga" and the "Theme from Ice Castles."

After her high school graduation, Idina attended New York University's Tisch School of the Arts, a college that attracted budding stage actors. A drama major, the freshman experienced dorm life while keeping her wedding singer job. She also wrote songs and pursued a record deal.

"NYU was a great school," Idina told *Stage Directions Magazine.* "It was all about wearing whatever you want, being unique and meeting interesting artists,"

Meanwhile Idina also altered her surname's spelling from Mentzel to Menzel. Because people always pronounced the silent T, she just omitted the letter entirely.

After earning a Bachelor of Fine Arts degree, Idina worked weddings and pursued music. As 1995 neared its end, she knew the upcoming months would be a sluggish time for weddings and worried about her bank account balance.

One evening a flyer posted at a small club caught her eye. New York Theatre Workshop, an off-Broadway venue that regularly presented new works, sought unknown performers for a forthcoming production. Little-known composer/lyricist Jonathan Larson had created an electrifying rock musical based on Puccini's *La bohème.*

What would it hurt to try out?

**BORN ENTERTAINER**
(A. Gilbert/PR Photos)

*"[Rent] is about living in the moment. 'No day but today.'"*

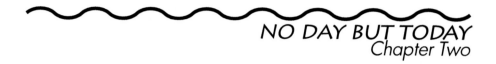

# NO DAY BUT TODAY
## Chapter Two

In early 1996 Al and Nanette's son Jonathan Larson began his 10th year as a struggling composer in New York City, a destination bursting with starving artists. The thirty-five-year-old supported his dream by waiting tables at SoHo's Moondance Diner three days a week. His affable personality brought smiles to many customers over the years, and he developed meaningful friendships with his coworkers, including Jesse L. Martin, a budding actor with immense charm and a smooth singing voice.

Over the years Jonathan watched sadly as many of his close friends lost their lives to AIDS, a human immune system disease. Feeling helpless, the anguished composer vowed to channel his grief into something productive by writing a musical as a tribute to his fallen loved ones.

In the late 1980s, Jonathan and playwright Billy Aronson began modernizing Giacomo Puccini's opera *La bohème*, a tale about young bohemians living in 1840s Paris. The team reset the famous story in New York City's Lower East Side. Renamed *Rent*, the modernized musical followed close-knit friends affected by poverty and AIDS. After Billy left the project due to creative differences, Jonathan assumed full control, composing the score, penning its lyrics and writing the script. He named many characters after his deceased friends and drew from his dire financial state to depict a starving artist's life.

Loner musician Roger falls for a sickly dancer named Mimi. His friends include a documentary filmmaker named Mark, philosopher professor Tom Collins and percussionist Angel. The protagonists battle Benny Coffin III, an ex-roommate who marries into money. Everyone but Mark carries some form of the AIDS virus.

Idina auditioned for Maureen Johnson, a self-absorbed performance artist who leaves Mark for Joanne, a wealthy lawyer. The alluring character sings two showstoppers, "Over the Moon" and a fierce duet entitled "Take Me or Leave Me."

"Casting Maureen was tricky," casting director Bernard Telsey remarked on the documentary *No Day But Today: The Story of Rent.* "The woman needed to have this incredible rock voice and had to really belt."

Strapped for money, Idina needed the gig badly, so she entered her first audition feigning confidence and sass. After greeting Jonathan and director Michael Greif, she launched into a scorching rendition of Bonnie Raitt's "Something To Talk About." The impressed men requested a second song, so she selected Percy Sledge's "When a Man Loves a Woman."

"Do you have anything in a ballad?" Jonathan asked.

Idina considered the 1966 classic a love song. Maybe the tune didn't sound like a traditional romantic ballad, but it was definitely about love. The desperate artist needed the job so she answered as Maureen might.

"That **is** a ballad," she replied icily.

The actress held her breath. Had she gone too far? Jonathan mulled over her saucy retort.

"Oh yeah," he admitted. "You're right."

After Idina left, her unruly aura lingered. Although she didn't fit Maureen's description, Jonathan really wanted her in *Rent*.

"Let's create [the role] around her," he suggested.

Meanwhile Idina's high school friend Adam Pascal also auditioned for *Rent*. The powerful rocker struggled to get a recording contract and needed money urgently. A few days later, he landed Roger, the lead role.

Six talented unknowns completed *Rent's* principal cast. Former Pajama Party member Daphne Rubin-Vega played Mimi, Jesse L. Martin portrayed Tom Collins and Anthony Rapp won the role of Mark. Rounding out the cast, Wilson Jermaine Heredia brought Angel to life, Taye Diggs played smarmy Benny and Fredi Walker joined the musical as Joanne.

The night before rehearsals started, Jonathan hosted a dinner for *Rent's* cast and crew. The elated composer sported a giddy grin all evening. Having just quit his service job, he felt like a real working artist.

"I wrote a show about my friends so that they would not be forgotten," he announced. "And so I toast you, my friends who are here, and those who are not."

"I'm so happy," he later told a friend. "I finally have a life in the theater."

New Directors/New Directions Series

# RENT
by JONATHAN LARSON
directed by MICHAEL GREIF

| | |
|---|---|
| Musical Director | Tim Weil |
| Choreographer | Marlies Yearby |
| Set Designer | Paul Clay |
| Costume Designer | Angela Wendt |
| Lighting Designer | Blake Burba |
| Sound Designer | Darron L. West |
| Dramaturg | Lynn M. Thomson |
| Musical Arranger | Steve Skinner |
| Casting Director | Bernard Telsey Casting |
| Assistant Director | Martha Banta |
| Original Concept/Additional Lyrics | Billy Aronson |
| Film | Tony Gerber |
| Production Manager | Susan R. White |
| Production Stage Manager | Crystal Huntington |
| Assistant Stage Manager | Catherine J. Haley |

## THE CAST
### (in order of appearance)

| | |
|---|---|
| Mark Cohen | Anthony Rapp |
| Roger Davis | Adam Pascal |
| Tom Collins | Jesse L. Martin |
| Benjamin Coffin III | Taye Diggs |
| Joanne Jefferson | Fredi Walker |
| Angel Schunard | Wilson Jermaine Heredia |
| Mimi Marquez | Daphne Rubin-Vega |
| Maureen Johnson | Idina Menzel |
| Mark's Mom, Alison, and others | Kristen Lee Kelly |
| Christmas caroler, Mr. Jefferson, a pastor, and others | Byron Utley |
| Mrs. Jefferson, woman with bags, and others | Gwen Stewart |
| Gordon, the man, and others | Timothy Britten Parker |
| Man with squeegee, a cop, and others | Gilles Chiasson |
| Paul, a cop, and others | Rodney Hicks |
| Alexi Darling, Roger's mom, and others | Aiko Nakasone |

## THE BAND

| | |
|---|---|
| Keyboards | Tim Weil |
| Bass | Steve Mack |
| Guitar | Kenny Brescia |
| Drums | Jeff Potter |
| Keyboards 2/Guitar 2 | Daniel A. Weiss |

**There will be one 10 minute intermission.**

NYTW's New Directors/New Directions series is generously sponsored
by Philip Morris Companies Inc.

First Performance: January 26, 1996

On *Rent's* first rehearsal, the cast began by singing "Seasons of Love," the musical's act two opener. Unbeknownst to them at the time, the song would become a breakout hit. Afterward Jonathan pulled Idina aside.

"I'm going to write something more fitting for you," he promised, as recounted in the book *Rent*. "This part is going to be much bigger, because I love what you do."

The composer's unnecessary gesture touched Idina. The singer felt honored that he would rewrite the role to highlight her strengths. Jonathan, Michael and she spent weeks creating melodies for Maureen's first solo.

Rehearsals thrived. The company bonded instantly, feeling like they'd known one another forever. One afternoon Anthony and Idina headed to a nearby restaurant for a snack.

"Anthony, what do you think this is?" she asked.

"I don't know what we're doing," he replied. "But whatever it is, it's going to be an event."

Several days later Jonathan invited Idina to lunch at Tompkins Square Park. They munched on sandwiches and discussed their creative dreams. Throughout the conversation, the singer marveled at the composer's optimistic personality.

"I know this is going to change your lives," he smiled.

Later as Idina and Fredi rehearsed their second act duet, Jonathan stopped them mid-performance.

"This song is totally wrong for you," he announced. "It doesn't show off your voices and personalities."

Right before dress rehearsals began, Jonathan called Idina over to his piano. She sang "When a Man Loves a Woman" in several different keys for him. That night the composer created a new song entitled "Take Me or Leave Me."

The women sang the new work the next day as Taye Diggs rehearsed a scene across the room. Suddenly the smitten actor studied Idina with great interest.

"Wow," he thought. "I should get to know her better."

As opening night approached, an overworked Jonathan began feeling discomfort and nausea. During one rehearsal he suddenly experienced sharp chest pain and labored breathing.

"Call 911," he told Michael. "I'm having a heart attack."

Jonathan staggered to the theater's lobby and lay on the floor, anticipating the ambulance's arrival. As the artist gasped for breath, he shook his head in disbelief. Adam and Anthony were singing lyrics about dying in America.

Later Jonathan sat in a hospital bed attached to an IV, an EKG and a breathing machine. Scared and weak, he wept and struggled to keep air in his lungs. Doctors claimed he had food poisoning, pumped his stomach and sent him home. Two days later the ailing composer visited a different ER and received a flu diagnosis. The worried artist couldn't shake the hunch that something felt very wrong.

On January 24, 1996, Jonathan attended *Rent's* final dress rehearsal. The sold-out show went smoothly, earning a prolonged standing ovation. Afterward theater's young prodigy granted *The New York Times* an interview. Then he went home to rest. As the thirty-five-year old prepared hot tea, he suddenly lost consciousness.

When paramedics arrived, Jonathan had already lost his life due to a tear in his aortic wall. His parents later learned that their son likely suffered from Marfan syndrome, a disorder of the body's connective tissue. Had he been diagnosed and undergone surgery, he'd have had an over 90% survival rate. Instead the gifted artist died ten days before his 36th birthday.

A distraught Brian Carmondy spent the morning phoning his roommate's family, friends and colleagues. Michael gathered *Rent*'s company for an emergency meeting, hoping to break the news to the cast before they heard it elsewhere. Like everyone else, Idina was gutted over her friend's death.

The tight cast wondered whether they would still give that evening's performance. Finally someone contacted Jonathan's shell-shocked parents, who were headed to New York. When asked about the musical's fate, his grief-stricken father uttered just five words.

"The show will go on," he choked out.

That night Idina and *Rent*'s cast performed an invite-only sing-through. Jonathan's parents, family and friends attended the somber event. When Adam launched into Roger's solo about yearning to create one great song before his young death, sobs echoed throughout the theater. Yet when the musical reached "La Vie Bohème," the joyous one act finale, everyone became overwhelmed by the musical's "No Day But Today" message. Electricity filled the theater as impassioned actors and audience members danced jubilantly to the composer's life-affirming score.

"Losing Jonathan caused the cast to band together to keep it vibrant, important and energetic," Idina told *The Virginian Pilot*. "We all embarked on a mission, not just a show. It took us out of being selfish and worrying about our careers to thinking about how important this show was for people to hear what he was trying to say."

On February 11, 1996, *The New York Times* published Jonathan's interview, detailing his untimely death and *Rent*'s *La bohème* connection. The massive exposure ignited ticket sales. At one point, Anthony Rapp entered the box office and helped frazzled workers take phone orders.

Two days later the cast gathered backstage before their opening night performance. Idina battled nerves, sorrow and excitement, while Daphne led the cast in a prayer. Then the company achieved a tremendous performance.

Nearly every reviewer gave *Rent* spectacular reviews, heralding the production's score, lyrics, book and cast. Even *The New York Times*' curmudgeonly Ben Brantley lavished praise.

"People who complain about the demise of the American musical have simply been looking in the wrong places," he declared. "Well done, Mr. Larson."

"The cast is terrific and blessed with voices of remarkable flexibility and strength," the reviewer continued. "Mr. Rapp gives the show its energetic motor; the golden-voiced Mr. Pascal its meditative soul and Ms. Rubin-Vega its affirmative sensuality. Mr. Martin, Ms. Walker, Mr. Heredia and Ms. Menzel are all performers of wit and emotional conviction."

If *Rent*'s ticket sales soared before its reviews, they skyrocketed after the accolades. When the musical's first month sold out, producers extended the run by a month and those seats sold out, too. The show had outgrown its tiny theater.

Jonathan always dreamed of becoming a successful composer. For weeks his parents, sister Julie and the show's producers worked to make his dream an actuality. On February 23, they announced that *Rent* would transfer to Broadway.

"The day that we heard it was moving to Broadway was very jubilant and exciting," Idina recalled in *No Day But Today*. "It was so big and important."

Designers began renovating the derelict Nederlander Theatre to host *Rent*'s Broadway run. Workers built larger sets for the new venue and replaced the building's decrepit chairs, walls and ceiling. Graphic designers even unveiled a new logo.

*Rent*'s Broadway transfer also ensured that Idina would receive a paycheck far greater than her previous $300.00 a week wage. Cast members successfully requested that every ac-

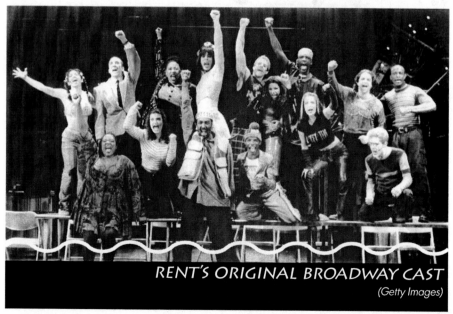

**RENT'S ORIGINAL BROADWAY CAST**
*(Getty Images)*

tor, principal or ensemble, receive the same salary. Idina could finally afford a comfortable apartment and other perks.

As *Rent's* live for today message resonated with theatergoers, Idina believed the show contained several messages.

"Live each day to its fullest," she told *Playbill.* "It's also about acceptance, tolerance and loving whoever you want."

On April 9th, the cast rehearsed for *Rent's* Broadway opening, while reporters and television cameras flooded the theater. Earlier that morning Columbia University had awarded Jonathan the Pulitzer Prize for Drama. The show became only the seventh musical to win the honor.

On April 29th, *Rent* celebrated its Broadway premiere. When Idina arrived at the Nederlander, reporters, photographers and curious bystanders jammed 41st Street. Celebrities waved their tickets at television cameras before hurrying into the venue. Notable attendees included George Clooney, Michelle Pfeiffer, Sigourney Weaver and David Geffen.

After Idina received several floral deliveries, she met her friends on stage. The emotional cast held hands and dedicated the opening night performance in Jonathan's memory.

Once again *Rent* received exceptional reviews. Critics praised Jonathan's intelligent lyrics, eclectic score and raw script. Idina also earned acclaim as the self-enamored performance artist.

"Idina Menzel brings new, welcome satiric shadings to her character's artistic affectations." – *The New York Times*

"*Rent* (is) a loud, fervent, energizing show that is a perfect wedding of music and subject." – *The Record*

"Idina Menzel and Fredi Walker roar "Take Me or Leave Me" with authority." – *The Washington Times*

Idina quickly became one of *Rent's* breakout stars. Her no frills personality and monstrous talent attracted many fans. Young girls especially idolized her.

"I don't feel like a star," she shrugged on *48 Hours*. "I just have this job with 14 other cool, really warm, talented people. We're all in this cozy ride together."

Meanwhile Idina harbored quite a crush on Taye, and he liked her, too. The couple flirted all the time. Sometimes the actress found Post-it notes on her dressing room mirror congratulating her on a great number. She nicknamed him Sandalwood because he smelled like the fragrance oil, and he called her Dee. One evening they went to see the newly released movie *Twister* and became an official couple.

Despite her theater success, Idina still dreamed of touring the world as a recording artist. On her day off, she played venues like CBGB's and the Bitter End, hoping a record executive might sign her.

On May 6, 1996, the Tony Awards announced theater's season best finalists. *Rent* nabbed ten nominations, including Best Musical, Direction, Choreography and Lighting Design. Jonathan also scored two posthumous nods, Best Book of a Musical and Best Original Score. And Adam, Daphne, Wilson and Idina secured acting nominations!

### Best Featured Actress In A Musical

Ann Duquesnay - *Bring in 'da Noise, Bring in 'da Funk*
Veanne Cox - *Company*
Joohee Choi - *The King and I*
Idina Menzel - *Rent*

The first-time nominee attended the *50th Annual Tony Awards* at the Majestic Theatre on June 2, 1996. Although Idina didn't win her category, she celebrated when *Rent* won Best Musical and Jonathan took two statuettes. The enthusiastic company also performed "Seasons of Love" and "La Vie Bohème" to great acclaim.

**IDINA & TAYE**
*(Tom Walck/PR Photos)*

Several weeks later Idina immortalized Maureen on *Rent's* original cast album. On a bonus track, the cast and international singing star Stevie Wonder recorded "Seasons of Love."

A few months later, Chelsea Clinton celebrated her 17th birthday with a New York excursion accompanied by her parents Bill and Hillary Clinton. The First Daughter begged her mother and father for *Rent* tickets and soon the world's most famous trio sat in Nederlander Theatre's fifth row, watching Broadway's biggest hit. During her character's painfully bad performance art, Idina embraced the opportunity to interact with the President of the United States.

"Come on, sir, moo with me!" the actress implored to the world's most powerful man,

A tickled President Clinton laughed and mooed back at Idina. Later he described the musical as "incredible" and "powerful." After the performance, *Rent's* cast sang "Happy Birthday" to Chelsea.

On July 1, 1997, during *Rent's* curtain call, Idina wiped away tears as she bid goodbye to the musical. The show still boasted record-breaking box office numbers, but its original Maureen felt ready to explore new avenues. Hollywood Records had signed her to a recording contract, and she looked forward to pursuing a solo career.

*"[Still I Can't Be Still] refers to serenity and the stillness within your soul."*

# IDINA CAN'T BE STILL
## Chapter Three

It happened! Idina's dream came true. Hollywood Records had signed her to a contract. She was officially a recording artist!

"I'm feeling bittersweet these days, as I've left *Rent* to pursue my lifelong dream of recording my own music," Idina told her online fan club. "While it was incredibly difficult to leave the show, I'm so excited to be embarking on my album."

On September 15, 1998, Hollywood Records released Idina's debut album entitled *Still I Can't Be Still*. The ambiguous title provoked much debate among music lovers and the singer's devoted fans. Throughout various press interviews, the performer expressed her thoughts on the name.

"It's a take on all the meanings of the word 'still,'" Idina told *CNN*. "Still, meaning serenity, calmness; and still, meaning more to come. It really stemmed from the fact that there were all these wonderful things happening for me while I was in *Rent*, and then given the opportunity to make my album. I was constantly unsatisfied, and through that stemmed probably a lot of the emotion in many of the songs."

The 11-track CD covered various themes, such as fear of aging ("Straw into Gold"), child abuse ("Larissa's Lagoon") and female empowerment ("Heart on My Sleeve"). Idina co-wrote every track with producer Milton Davis and recorded the album at historic Bearsville Studios near Woodstock, New York, which previously hosted artists like The Rolling Stones and R.E.M. *Rent* costar Gwen Stewart provided background vocals on three songs.

In the CD's acknowledgments, Idina first thanked her mother, father and sister. Plus Jonathan Larson, her *Rent* family and all her faithful fans also received recognition. Finally, she closed the section by thanking Taye, her soul mate.

Earlier that summer Idina received enormous exposure when concert promoters invited her to perform *Still I Can't Be Still's* songs during select Lilith Fair dates. Founded by Sarah McLachlan, the tour showcased female artists with proceeds going toward women's rights organizations.

Prior to her first performance, Idina waited backstage anxiously. Two years had passed since her *Rent* debut. The nervous performer worried that people might have forgotten her. When the announcer called her name, she stepped into the spotlight's harsh glare and heard rapturous cheers.

"Go, Idina," squealed some girls.

"We love you, Idina," shouted others.

The supportive gestures made the artist teary-eyed. Her loyal following always exceeded her dreams. She felt so blessed.

"Wow, it's been a long time, but they have stuck with me!" Idina thought.

Throughout the tour, the grateful artist enjoyed meeting admirers. Some people ran websites devoted to her, while others had seen *Rent* over 30 times. Meanwhile Idina met her own musical heroes, like Sarah McLachlan, Natalie Merchant, Bonnie Raitt and Des'ree.

**HALLOWEEN CONCERT**
*(Stephen Cohen/PR Photos)*

Upon *Still I Can't Be Still's* release, it received many favorable reviews. Idina's strong vocals and multi-layered interpretations drew high praise. Some music professionals compared the singer/songwriter to multi-platinum star Tori Amos and Grammy winner Alanis Morissette.

"The singer spends her time torn between what's good for her and what feels good to her, delivering sharply worded songs in a powerful, keening voice." - *The Washington Post*

"[Idina] shows off a smoky, penetrating alto and a facility for writing rock-and soul-inflected tunes." - *The Boston Herald*

"Minuet" marked *Still I Can't Be Still's* first single. In the catchy tune about Taye, Idina worries that her sloppy habits might chase her boyfriend away. Later she sings that she wants to someday marry him.

One morning Idina and visitor Daphne-Rubin Vega spent the morning chatting while technicians prepared the set for "Minuet's" music video. Shortly after production began, workers discovered that a beat-up Volkswagen, a major element in the video, had faulty windows that would not close. As a result, Idina and costar Taye filmed the entire shoot with water spraying onto them. By day's end, they were drenched!

Despite the mishap the video looked great. In the black and white piece, Idina daydreams about her boyfriend while lounging in a van at a car wash. The famous couple played guitar, kissed, sang and had a pillow fight.

"Minuet" didn't become a Top 40 hit, but it reached #48 on Radio & Records' CHR/Pop tracks chart. The video also received modest airplay on independent video channels.

Meanwhile Taye's film career catapulted after winning the male lead opposite Oscar nominee Angela Bassett in *How Stella Got Her Groove Back*. Idina gamely walked the red carpet at the movie's premiere. Dressed in a colorful sundress and shades, she radiated happiness for her boyfriend's success!

Later that year Idina appeared on *VH1's* series *Midnight Minute*. Every midnight the show gave a musical artist 60 seconds to perform selections from their new album. The innovative show featured performers like Alanis Morissette, Sixpence None the Richer, Duncan Sheik and Long Island's favorite former wedding singer!

In November of 1998, Idina kicked off her first concert tour in Alexandria, Virginia. Over the next few months, the singer and her four-member band played major markets, such as New York, Ohio, Pennsylvania and California. Her fans appeared at every stop, and she earned new followers, too.

Idina was living her dream. Every night she played her original music at a concert venue. Sometimes she glanced into the crowd just to watch a fan singing along to her lyrics. It thrilled her.

"This is what I've always wanted," Idina told the *Albany Times Union*. "I'm trying to embrace it. I'm bad at enjoying the moment. I really am. *Still I Can't Be Still*, you know?"

*"The more you challenge yourself, the more interesting a human being and an artist you'll be."*

## LIFE OF THE PARTY
### Chapter Four

In February of 2000, Idina returned to musical theater in an original off-Broadway musical called *The Wild Party*. Based on Joseph Moncure March's narrative poem, the story follows a wealthy couple named Queenie and Burrs who throw a liquor-filled party during the 1920s Jazz prohibition-era. Throughout the evening's dangerous course, the pair's colorful friends arrive and add flavor to the social gathering, which ends in tragedy. Featuring music, book and lyrics by Andrew Lippa, the limited-engagement played the Manhattan Theatre Club, a company known for producing innovative works.

Idina stole the show nightly as Kate, Queenie's (Julia Murney) outrageous rival. Meanwhile, Taye's Mr. Black and Brian d'Arcy James' Burrs battled for Queenie's affections. A talented group completed the production's small ensemble.

Idina scored the musical's showiest numbers. The blaring "Look at Me Now" punctuated Kate's over-the-top entrance, while "The Juggernaut" showed her dance skills and mighty voice. Admirers craved for the belter to demonstrate her incomparable vocal acrobatics, and she delivered with the rousing "Life of the Party" and the "Let Me Drown" duet.

Idina loved *The Wild Party*'s twenty cast members. She especially adored working with Taye every night. They cherished the rare opportunity to spend so much time together. The singer also formed strong friendships with Julia and Brian.

If the cast gelled off-stage, they positively sizzled on stage. The talented group featured theater's finest actors, dancers and singers. Each night the hard-working company committed to the high-intensity show like they were performing it for the first time. The group formed a potent chemistry.

Meanwhile the actress loved playing her vulgar character. Like Maureen, Kate behaved however she wanted. In every performance, Idina elicited gasps from the audience when delivering her character's shocking quips or eye-popping stunts. She loved portraying the musical's outlandish screwball.

"This is the best role I've played in a long while," Idina told *Theatre.com*. "It's fun, risky and challenging."

*Curtain Up* heaped countless compliments on the show by remarking, "There are several show-stoppers that make you want to own the CD. The performers deserve their star billing -- Julia Murney as the wide-eyed Queenie, Brian d'Arcy James as the cruel and conflicted Burrs, Taye Diggs as the mysterious and smitten-with-Queenie Black and Idina Menzel as the anything-for-kicks Kate."

As incredible coincidence would have it, a different *Wild Party* opened that season. Composer Michael John LaChiusa and librettist George C. Wolfe lured Oscar nominee Toni Collette into making her Broadway debut as Queenie in their rendition of March's poem. Mandy Patinkin played the manic Burrs, while Eartha Kitt, Marc Kudisch and Tonya Pinkins completed the cast. Sadly the show drew anemic ticket sales and closed after only 68 performances.

Meanwhile, the celebration continued nightly off-Broadway at Lippa's *Wild Party*. Idina and the company felt overjoyed with overwhelming box office results. Theatergoers seemed eager to catch the famous performers in an intimate setting. The popular show even added an extra week to its limited run.

Working as a New York stage actress might sound highly glamorous, but Idina lived a fairly quiet life. Every morning she drank tea and ate cereal before heading to the gym. Following rehearsal or voice lessons, the performer took a nap. Afterward she warmed up her voice and headed to the theater. When the exhausted star returned home five hours later, she ate a snack while watching television.

*The Wild Party* scooped up several top honors that theater season. The Drama Desk Awards honored the musical with 12 nods. Idina also received an acting nomination.

Although some speculated that *The Wild Party* might make a Broadway transfer, its producers claimed the proposed move made little financial sense. Nevertheless, the show gained a fervid following. On April 11, the company assembled at Edison Recording Studios to commemorate the show with a cast recording, hoping a CD would inspire future theaters to produce the musical.

"*The Wild Party* deserves a longer life," Idina told *Theatre.com*. "More people need to hear it. If that means we document it on a CD, that's the best thing we could do."

After *The Wild Party* closed, Idina found herself in high demand. She often turned down enticing projects, like a musical workshop of *Bright Lights, Big City* directed by *Rent*'s Michael Greif and featuring friends Daphne-Rubin Vega and Anthony Rapp. The brash New York-based musical seemed like an ideal fit for the powerhouse vocalist.

Except the judicious performer chose a more subdued role instead, headlining *Summer of '42*. In the musical based on Herman Raucher's book, teenager Hermie falls for a war bride who teaches the young boy a lesson in love.

Idina traveled to picturesque Chester, Connecticut, for *Summer of '42*'s run at the Goodspeed Opera House. The stage diva loved performing David Kirshenbaum's lovely score in the intimate 200-seat Norma Terris Theatre. She felt honored to belt the show's best songs, including soaring solos like "Losing Track of Time" and "Our Story So Far."

The tiny, eight-actor musical opened on August 10 to great fanfare. Theatergoers gobbled up tickets, so producers added an additional week. Due to its great interest, the show also booked an October engagement at Dayton, Ohio's Victoria Theatre, which also produced remarkable business. Idina had established herself as a big box office draw.

Around the same time, Idina and Taye became engaged! The joyful bride-to-be often spent her days enjoying Connecticut's idyllic scenery while planning her dream wedding. Unlike many women Idina welcomed her fiancés' input.

"I definitely have a say," Taye told *The Washington Informer*. "We discuss what we want and then she makes the phone calls. So, it's okay, so far."

"It'll be very personal," he added. "Very small."

Before Idina walked down the aisle, though, she stepped back onto the Broadway stage as a replacement performer in Disney's *Aida*. With music by Sir Elton John and lyrics by Tim Rice, the musical spun the classic tale of forbidden love between enslaved Nubian princess Aida and Egyptian soldier Radames. Taye's fiancée succeeded 1980s sensation Taylor Dayne as insecure, fashion-obsessed Princess Amneris.

Idina sang several thrilling songs including the opener "Every Story is a Love Story" which sets the show's chilling mood. She also breathed life into "My Favorite Suit," a delightful Motown-inspired crowd pleaser and the heartbreaking "I Know the Truth."

Idina's appearance reunited her with good friend Adam Pascal who played Radames. Every night the grateful star walked to the Palace Theatre in Times Square and counted her blessings. She felt honored to belong to New York's theater community. However, as much as she loved playing Amneris, she couldn't help wishing she could someday create another new role.

As fate would have it, all the way across the country, composer Stephen Schwartz worked furiously on a new musical. The show would become a gigantic blockbuster.

And Idina? Well she would star in it.

*"[Elphaba's] very vulnerable and fragile. She's gotten a bad rap."*

# THE WIZARD & IDINA
## Chapter Five

On January 11, 2003, Idina and her best friend were married at the Round Hill resort in Montego Bay, Jamaica. The bride floated down the rose petal-covered aisle toward a beaming Taye and joined him under a white canopy. Their hands intertwined, the duo exchanged vows in an intimate nighttime setting overlooking the Caribbean Sea. After the ecstatic couple shared their first kiss as husband and wife, Stevie Wonder's "Overjoyed" serenaded them.

The small wedding party dressed elegantly. Idina wore a white strapless Bagley Mishka gown with ornate crystal beading and a delicate floor-length veil. White blossoms decorated her brunette tresses, which she gathered in an upswept hairstyle. The groom sported an-off white John Varvatos suit and bridesmaids donned beige dresses with gypsy-style skirts.

After the ceremony husband and wife greeted family and friends at the hotel's gorgeous terrace. Partygoers, like Daphne-Rubin Vega, celebrated to an eclectic musical set list, while sampling a scrumptious five-tier wedding cake embellished with leaves and pale yellow roses.

Back in New York City, theater lovers celebrated the announcement of Idina's return to Broadway later that year in a brand-new musical called *Wicked*. The production's future home, the enormous Gershwin Theatre, reported record-breaking ticket sales.

## THE HAPPY COUPLE
(Albert L. Ortega/PR Photos)

Eight years earlier, Oscar-winner Stephen Schwartz and friends enjoyed a relaxing Hawaiian vacation. On a sailing excursion, he noticed his buddy Holly Near sitting silently by herself. Engrossed in a book, the singer-songwriter seemed oblivious to the merriment surrounding her.

"What are you reading?" Stephen asked.

"*Wicked* by Gregory Maguire," she replied, not looking at him.

Suddenly the woman stopped reading and studied the composer. Her eyes danced with inspiration.

"This book would make a great musical," she exclaimed.

"What's it about?" he replied.

Holly got comfy and gushed about the acclaimed novel. Maguire created a *Wizard of Oz* prologue told from the Wicked Witch of the West's perspective. The author painted the green witch as a misunderstood, sympathetic outsider. And Glinda the Good Witch? Well she wasn't so saccharine sweet.

The composer listened in wonderment. The premise sounded like the best musical premise he had ever heard. He instantly envisioned the green witch Elphaba taking flight in the first act finale. Chorus numbers rang in his head.

When he returned home, the giddy composer bought the book and learned that Universal Pictures retained its rights. Actress Demi Moore wanted to star in a film version. Months later, though, the studio changed their minds and offered to produce Stephen's stage musical.

*Wicked* follows *The Wizard of Oz's* supporting characters long before Dorothy Gale arrives in Emerald City. An insecure loner named Elphaba, also known as the Wicked Witch of the West, meets spoiled, popular Galinda (later Glinda) at Shiz University. As different as night and day, the girls form an improbable friendship. When the green-skinned heroine uncovers the Wizard's devious plot to end animal rights, she embarks on a brave mission to save her furry friends. Along the way, Elphaba and Glinda also battle one another for the affections of dim-witted hunk Fiyero.

Stephen Schwartz handled *Wicked's* score and lyrics. An earlier multi-tasking project landed him a Best Song Academy Award for *The Prince of Egypt's* "When You Believe" to accompany his two Oscars for *Pocahontas.* Emmy-winning writer Winnie Holzman assumed book duties, while Joe Mantello came aboard as director.

Having read Maguire's book, Idina yearned to play Elphaba. She entered her audition dressed as a Goth girl, wearing green eye shadow, green lipstick, black biker boots and a dark dress. The singer aced the lengthy audition process and earned the coveted role.

"I just felt really connected and attached to this character," Idina told *The British Theatre Guide.* "I related to the dark, grungy girl who didn't quite fit in."

Meanwhile, Tony-winner Kristin Chenoweth would play Glinda. *Rent* alumnus Norbert Leo Butz joined the cast as handsome Fiyero, and *Mad Men's* Robert Morse signed to play the Wizard. Finally Carole Shelley planned to terrorize the leading ladies nightly as the devious Madame Morrible.

© Getty Images | Image is subject to copyright

*AS ELPHABA IN WICKED*
(Getty Images)

"I see [my role] as a really strong supporting character, but it is a great part," Kristin told *Playbill.* "(Stephen's) music is fantastic. Yeah, I wish that I had more to sing, but I took it for the journey that this character takes."

"Originating a role in theater is pretty great," Idina remarked. "I was sitting at a piano with Stephen Schwartz and being a mouthpiece for his thoughts and imagination. That's fun for me."

Idina flew to San Francisco in early 2003. *Wicked* would play Northern California for a month, ironing any wrinkles before heading to Broadway. The actress took a deep breath before embarking on the most difficult, rewarding experience of her career.

On May 28, 2003, *Wicked* held its world premiere at the Curran Theatre. Cast and crew slaved over the show in rehearsals and felt anxious to gauge an audience's reaction.

Despite the company's nerves, *Wicked* enjoyed a sensational opening night. The enthusiastic audience flipped for the musical's gifted cast, heartwarming story and gigantic sets. Crowds at intermission even flooded the souvenir stand, requesting a cast album that hadn't been recorded yet!

During that night's curtain call, the show's leading ladies walked center stage to take their bow. Kristin looked out into the audience and discovered everyone standing and applauding fervently. The petite blonde gasped. Although the actress owned a Tony award, she'd never starred in a successful show.

"Oh my gosh," Kristin exclaimed to her costar. "I've never been in a show that got a standing ovation!"

Idina laughed and then affectionately squeezed Kristin's hand. Having experienced *Rent*'s popularity, the performer knew all about standing ovations. She felt thrilled to share the precious moment with her friend.

Thankfully critics liked the show, too, especially its bright stars. "*Wicked* is absolutely magical," raved *The Oakland Post*. "Menzel's voice is huge and is characterized by clear phrasing, solid intonation, direct communication." Meanwhile *The Oakland Tribune* saluted the musical's score, sets, special effects and its talented cast, citing Idina's work as "outstanding."

Despite its strong reception, *Wicked*'s cast and crew continued revising the show during its out-of-town tryout. Winnie trimmed twenty fives minutes from the script. Stephen continually altered songs, switching up lyrics and even melodies. Through it all, Idina reacted like a fearless leader.

Idina was such a trouper," Stephen raved to the *San Francisco Chronicle*. "She impressed me so much because she had the lion's share of the changes. Sometimes we would go to certain actors and give them three new lines and they'd say, 'Well, I don't know if I can get this in tonight.' And Idina would have whole new scenes she had to throw in, and she'd say, 'I'll get it in there for you. I'll do my best.' And then she'd run backstage in the brief time she had offstage and read her lines over for the next scene and run out and do it."

Prior to *Wicked*'s New York debut, the creative team finalized several key changes. Joel Grey assumed the powerful Wizard role. Norbert's smooth vocals and devilish demeanor inspired Stephen to replace "Which Way's the Party?" with "Dancing Through Life." Plus the casting department recast some minor roles. Through it all, though, the entire team retained the show's numerous messages.

"*Wicked* is multi-thematic," Idina told *Playbill*. "The show is about finding out who you truly are. It's about race and propaganda. And it's about the friendship between these two women. How many shows can you think of in which two women characters really care about each other? It's rare."

*Wicked's* arduous score demanded more from Idina than any other performer. Throughout the musical the singer sang six major songs. Each work was incredibly difficult and represented a completely different musical style.

The lead's first solo defines Stephen's trademark 'I want' opener. In the composer's shows, his characters begin their journey by expressing what they desire more than anything. In the soaring "The Wizard and I" the green heroine expresses her wish to meet the Wizard, wrongly believing that he can solve problems that stem from her unusual looks. The solo premieres the oft-repeated unlimited theme that contains the first seven notes of "Over the Rainbow," an homage that well-trained musical ears picked up quickly.

In "I'm Not That Girl" the outcast expresses the painful realization that she'll never be the traditional pretty girl, like her best friend Glinda. The song quickly became an anthem for young girls struggling to accept what they perceived as their physical imperfections.

"Defying Gravity" shows the main character spurning a promised life of acceptance in favor of helping her friends in need. Using a book of spells, she takes flight, literally, while finally embracing her uniqueness. Audiences gasp in astonishment as Elphaba flies high above the stage to end act one. The breathtaking sequence recalls thrilling theatrical moments like *Miss Saigon's* helicopter, *The Phantom of the Opera's* chandelier or *Les Misérables'* barricade. The song marked Idina's favorite number.

In "As Long as You're Mine" Elphaba finds true love. Sung as a duet with boyfriend Fiyero, the couple expresses their affection for one another. Idina loved singing the soulful number because for the first time in her career, she got to be the ingénue!

"No Good Deed" marks the musical's most vocally demanding number, one that comes two plus hours into the show, after its singer has performed four grueling numbers and flown high above the stage. During Elphaba's angry tirade, she experiences a near meltdown after losing everything

**"ELPHABA" AND "FIYERO"**
(Janet Mayer/PR Photos)

that has mattered to her. The tune also features several tongue twister phrases that double as witches' spells. Idina claimed the tricky language came easier for her thanks to having had a bat mitzvah.

The lead women close their musical journey every night with "For Good," a ballad that celebrates friendship. The song occurs near the show's thrilling climax. Elphaba and Glinda must say goodbye to one another, knowing they will never meet again. Idina loved singing the song nightly. She felt awe at how two different voices blended so perfectly.

During *Wicked*'s development stages, Stephen struggled writing "For Good" more than any other song. Could he write a song about losing a best friend? How would he, as man in his late 40s, possibly understand the dynamics of two young

## WICKED SIGNING
*(Melissa Siuty)*

women saying goodbye? Frustrated, he turned to his teenage daughter Jessica for help.

"What would you tell your best friend if you were never going to see her again?" he asked.

The young girl contemplated her father's question. Her mind wandered to her lifelong friend Jessie. The prospect of losing the friendship brought tears to her eyes. Finally, Jessica answered that she would tell her friend that fate had brought them together and Jessie filled a void in her life. She would apologize for any pain she caused her and would always feel changed by their friendship.

Stephen sat overwhelmed for a moment. Jessica's insight and eloquence floored him.

"Thank you," he answered emotionally.

A few moments later, the composer returned to his office and resumed work on the song with a fresh perspective. Several days later he'd finished "For Good." Besides "Defying Gravity," the piece became the show's biggest hit.

"It's the only time where we're not acting," Idina revealed. "As friends and as women, we are connected and realize that it's an important message to be getting out there."

With *Wicked*'s strong friendship theme, Idina felt relieved that she and Kristin connected so effortlessly. The women shared spectacular chemistry on stage, and they adored each other off-stage.

"I like Idina so much that it's hard for me to be mean to her," Kristin remarked. "I have to put my feelings aside."

"You couldn't do it unless you had admiration for one other," Idina told *PBS Theater Talk*. "I'm envious of her wonderful qualities. There's so much to learn from her onstage and off stage. It's been a life experience."

Due to the diverse, difficult score, *Wicked*'s team felt thrilled to have Idina on board. The dynamic singer gamely handled the show's vocal demands. *Rent* and *Wicked*'s casting agent Bernard Telsey lavished praise on the leading lady.

"I remember the days when Maureen seemed tricky in *Rent*," he gushed. "Well, Maureen is Elphaba plus, because Maureen sings one song and Elphaba sings six. And you're the star. You don't have to carry the show as Maureen."

On October 30th, *Wicked* opened on Broadway. Wild enthusiasm greeted the show. Each song received rapturous applause. Clever dialogue drew much laughter.

At the opening night party, Idina wore a silver gown that showcased her slim figure. Sporting an elegant hair bun, she greeted admirers at Central Park's famed Tavern in the Green restaurant. She felt thrilled that her parents and sister stood by her side. Throughout the evening, people commended her remarkable performance. Critics were also impressed.

"Elphaba is played superbly by Menzel, with a fierce, gripping intensity that still allows us to see the vulnerability underneath." – *The Record*.

"Menzel is a winning presence. She's a thrilling belter. She powers through the brawny ballads with a gusto that raises goose bumps, especially in the Act 1 finale, "Defying Gravity," in which the sky is literally her limit." – *The Washington Post*

"The tall and beautiful Ms. Menzel makes a brilliantly complex and sympathetic Elphaba. Her big numbers raise the roof." – *The New York Observer*

Patti LuPone as *Evita*, Sarah Brightman in *The Phantom of the Opera* and *Miss Saigon*'s Lea Salonga – all three women delivered iconic performances. Those stage legends, however, only played their parts six times a week. Producers used a standby to play the remaining two performances, letting the stars rest their voices.

Idina, on the other hand, eschewed the standby option. Despite the role's enormous difficulty, the dynamic singer performed all eight scheduled shows a week. She even boasted a stellar attendance record. Grandmothers, grown men, little girls – many of them dreamed of watching the popular performer. The compassionate entertainer wouldn't disappoint them, especially given steep ticket prices.

Because *Wicked* required much oomph, Idina lived a low-key life, saving her energy for the musical. After every evening performance, she went straight home, ordered food and watched television. Her favorite guilty pleasure? *The Bachelorette*. She also loved tennis and never missed a major tournament. On her one day off, the trained singer didn't speak, giving her voice a necessary break.

Playing Elphaba required the actress to sport the witch's trademark skin color. Makeup artists took MAC cosmetic's green color, added water and applied the mixture using a Japanese brush. The process took approximately 40 minutes. To ensure the actress didn't sweat off the makeup during the strenuous show, the crew used a fixing spray to keep it from running. After the show ended, Idina removed the color by showering with a specific water pressure and scrubbing her skin with Neutrogena.

Despite her best efforts, though, Idina didn't always successfully remove her green makeup. Occasionally she missed a few spots. Several times the actress would be at an important social event and noticed people studying her face.

"You left some green makeup on," they'd finally say!

On December 16, Decca Broadway released *Wicked's* Original Broadway Cast Recording. The 19-track CD became a best seller, reaching double platinum status. It even won a 2005 Grammy Award for Best Musical Show Album.

At the end of 2003, Idina received an unexpected Christmas gift when Taye played Fiyero for a four-week stint. Norbert threw out his back and needed a month to recover. As producers scrambled for a replacement, Idina had a brilliant idea.

While wrapping the feature film *Drum* in South Africa, Taye felt anxious to return home. He missed his wife dearly. Suddenly his cell phone rang.

"Norbert injured his back," Idina announced. "He'll miss the show for at least four weeks."

"That's terrible," her husband replied.

"You might be mad about it, but I suggested you to replace him," she said.

A few days later, Taye sat on a New York-bound plane clutching *Wicked's* script. When he arrived at the Gershwin Theatre, he learned the show's blocking and choreography in

ASK THE DUST PREMIERE
(David Gabber/PR Photos)

four days. Then he tackled Fiyero's two songs and attended costume fittings.

On December 22, 2003, Taye made his *Wicked* debut opposite his favorite leading lady. He and Idina sparkled as star-crossed lovers, particularly in their romantic duet. Internet users, magazines and newspapers buzzed about the couple's first Broadway pairing since *Rent*.

"I'm so excited about him joining," Idina gushed to *Playbill*. "It'll be just great for the holidays, and we can spend time together, and I think he's perfect for the role. But I miss Norbert tremendously."

Throughout the show's sold-out run, many notable people attended performances. Tom Cruise stopped by one evening, and Nicole Kidman caught a matinee. Margaret O'Brien's godson visited and gave Idina his godmother's black gloves from *The Wizard of Oz* film.

Although Idina loved meeting so many celebrities, she felt especially honored to perform for *Wicked*'s young fans. Children and teens loved the message that uniqueness should be celebrated. When the actress left the theater every night, fans waited to meet her. Many expressed how the show eased their pain and insecurities over being an outsider.

"Be different is cool," Idina stressed when signing autographs. "Don't change for anyone."

When awards season kicked off, *Wicked* swiped ten Tony Award nominations, including Best Musical, Best Score and Best Book. Its two stars would also attend the prestigious award show as nominees.

## **Best Performance by a Leading Actress in a Musical**
Kristin Chenoweth - *Wicked*
Stephanie D'Abruzzo - *Avenue Q*
Idina Menzel - *Wicked*
Donna Murphy - *Wonderful Town*
Tonya Pinkins - *Caroline, or Change*

On the morning of the Tony Awards, Idina attended camera rehearsal for "Defying Gravity" the number she and Kristin would perform at the event. Afterward, she attended yoga class to help her achieve a relaxed state. The actress had not prepared a speech, not expecting to win. As she left class, her agent emailed her.

"Don't be your self-deprecating self and not be prepared," she wrote. "Write a speech. There's a chance you could win."

When Idina arrived home, nerves overwhelmed her. She lay on her bed next to a napping Taye. He awoke and held his crying wife.

"Everybody's telling me to write a speech, but I don't want to," she admitted. "I don't want to get my hopes up."

"Who cares?" he urged. "Let's get our hopes up, and if it doesn't happen, it doesn't happen."

The couple sat opposite one another as Taye coached his wife through an acceptance speech. Idina looked lovingly at her husband. She felt so grateful for his support and friendship.

Hours later Idina and Taye arrived at Radio City Music Hall. The stunning actress wore a violet chiffon halter gown. She waved to screaming fans assembled outside the historic theater before walking inside to enjoy the fruits of her labor.

Nearly three hours later, Renee Zellweger and director Rob Marshall literally danced onto the stage hand in hand. The talented artists, who worked with Taye on *Chicago*, would present Best Actress in a Musical.

"And the Tony award goes to Idina Menzel!"

*Wicked's* popular leading lady took a moment to compose herself before she kissed her husband and headed to the stage. An emotional Taye wept, while Kristin beamed for her friend. Despite being shocked by her victory, Idina delivered a truly memorable acceptance speech.

> "I'm so proud to be in a musical that celebrates women – that celebrates their strengths and their differences. To be in the company of these women this evening is just a dream for me. Thank you so much.
>
> Kristin Chenoweth, you are the grace and the light on that stage every night. This is something we built together and I love you.
>
> Joe Mantello has had the faith in me for three and a half years and kicked my butt into this role. Stephen Schwartz for writing some of the most beautiful music a girl can sing eight times a week. Winnie Holzman for giving the green girl a heart.
>
> My mother, my father, sister Cara and grandmother, who are here tonight. Thank you for taking me to see *Dreamgirls* and *Annie*.
>
> And my beautiful, beautiful husband who tells me he loves me every time I feel like the biggest loser. I love you so much.
>
> Thank you, everybody."

Two weeks later, Idina took a 17-day break from playing Elphaba to fly to South Africa. The devoted artist had accepted a film role in Robert Towne's *Ask the Dust*. Colin Farrell and Salma Hayek headed the cast, while she played Vera, a woman smitten with the leading man's character.

"I get to spend two weeks kissing Colin Farrell. But it's nothing compared to kissing Taye Diggs," she quipped.

In her first major movie role, critics gave Idina great reviews. She established herself as a natural actress on film.

"Menzel trembles with vulnerability; it makes you want to see her in films more often." – *The Associated Press*

"More touching is Idina Menzel as a woman coming apart and helpless to stop it." – *The Christian Science Monitor*

"It was great," Idina laughed. "I got to stop wearing the green makeup."

The Broadway star returned to *Wicked* just in time to bid goodbye to Kristin who left the show to pursue film opportunities. *Urinetown*'s Jennifer Laura Thompson took over as Glinda. The newest cast member expressed admiration at her costar's incredible popularity.

"It really does (feel like a rock concert), especially for Idina," Jennifer told *Playbill*. "People are there specifically to see her...crazy screaming. It's amazing!"

All great things eventually end, though. *Wicked*'s producers announced January 9, 2005, as Idina's final performance. In the matinee before her last day, disaster struck. During Elphaba's melting scene, a trap door opened prematurely and the actress plunged several feet through the opening. Audience members watched as paramedics rescued the injured actress.

Thirty minutes later, Idina lay in an ER bed holding her side in pain when a doctor entered the room. After the physician ordered x-rays, she looked at the actress still wearing her costume and green makeup.

"How should we remove this dress?" she mused.

"Rip it off," Idina replied.

"How much is it?" the dubious doctor asked.

"It's $20,000," the actress answered exasperatedly. "Who cares? These guys are making a lot of money!"

In the end, the physician refused to cut the gown. Three hospital workers ultimately removed the costume without causing any damage.

Doctors diagnosed Idina with a broken rib. When she returned home, her apartment resembled a flower shop. The Tony winner would miss her final show.

The next day Shoshana Bean gave a tremendous performance, but disappointed theatergoers felt sad about missing Idina's last show. However in the musical's closing moments, the Tony winner, wearing a red tracksuit, walked cautiously onto the stage. The ecstatic audience jumped to their feet, offering a nearly five-minute standing ovation before the beloved actress resumed the show by performing Elphaba's final scene.

"I love you all," she said at the curtain call. "It's been the best year of my life. Thank you."

Idina then returned home to recover. In her spare time, she chilled with her dog Sammy Davis Jr. and cats Ella and Coltrane. The actress stroked her pets while carefully studying a script. Soon she would film the movie version of the role that started it all!

**TONY WINNER**
*(Andrew Evans/PR Photos)*

*"Working with [Taye] was great! It was fun to see each other in the costumes that we were wearing when we were flirting in the first place."*

## RENT THE MOVIE
### Chapter Six

In late 2004 Columbia Pictures announced that the long-awaited *Rent* movie would hit theaters the following year. Several high profile names had been attached to the project over the years. Spike Lee and Martin Scorsese both wanted to direct at different stages, while recording artists Justin Timberlake and Christina Aguilera were courted as stars. In the end, Christopher Columbus, who helmed two *Harry Potter* features, won the daunting task of bringing the beloved musical to the silver screen.

While Idina performed on Broadway in *Wicked*, her agent Bonnie called her one afternoon. *Rent's* director had requested a meeting with the actress. In fact, he wanted to interview every original cast member.

"You're in the running for Maureen," Bonnie exclaimed.

Exhilaration bolted through Idina's body. Over the years she'd heard rumblings of a *Rent* movie but the names bandied about for the cast were major celebrities. Never did she dream that the director would consider her for a high-profile role. Insecurity and doubt quickly set in.

"He doesn't have to waste his time on me," she replied. "He's probably just being nice."

When Idina arrived at the meeting at Bonnie's insistence, Christopher studied her carefully. He knew she had the singing and acting chops for the role, but he'd wondered if she could pass for a young Bohemian on film. The director smiled in disbelief. How was it possible that nearly 10 years later, the original Maureen looked better than when she first performed in the show? The role was hers – again.

In early March 2005, the director announced *Rent*'s roster. Six original cast members would reprise their Broadway parts: Idina, Taye, Adam Pascal, Anthony Rapp, Jesse L. Martin and Wilson Jermaine Heredia. Original Broadway company member Daphne Rubin Vega was expecting a baby, while Fredi Walker, the original Joanne, was deemed too mature looking to recreate her role on celluloid. Rosario Dawson would play Mimi and Tracie Thoms joined the cast as Joanne.

"Because of the death of Jonathan, these people were forced to bond together in a way that I had just never seen," Christopher Columbus explained to *Playbill*. "There's a con-

RENT: THE MOTION PICTURE
(Sony Pictures)

nection there and a chemistry there that you just couldn't recreate. They needed to be in this film."

Production took place in New York, San Francisco and Los Angeles. Upon arriving on the set, Idina felt instantly comfortable and excited to retell Jonathan's vision.

"It was wonderful. It was like old times," she told *Playbill*. "It was very nostalgic. We have this way with one another where we fall right back into these dynamics that we always had. Taye's the funny one, (I'm) the flaky one, Jesse's always singing. We're a family. It was easy and felt very comfortable. It was really rewarding."

In late May the cast filmed the iconic "La Vie Bohème." The complicated sequence took five days to shoot, as the company performed the song again and again. When the scene wrapped, Idina returned to her hotel room and collapsed.

Several days later the actress shot Maureen's "Over the Moon" which she performed live. Christopher called the scene the shoot's most difficult challenge. He spent more time filming the song than any other, wanting to ensure that the awful performance art wouldn't alienate the audience.

"How bad of a performer should Maureen be?" the director asked in *Rent*'s DVD running commentary. "If she was too over the top, too flighty and not good enough, the audience wouldn't believe her. What's the point of Benny being concerned about her protest if she's not a good performer... not a talented performer? How is she going to possibly change things? So we had to work on that for quite some time."

"She's so committed," Anthony Rapp raved. "She's a little bit ironic but also very passionate. That's what makes it work."

Despite the exhausting schedule, Idina loved revisiting Maureen. She'd missed playing the conceited character.

"It's funny, having been away from Maureen for so long, I wasn't sure how well I knew her anymore," she wrote on *RentBlog.com*. "I didn't want to lose what drew people to her but there was more to discover. She is still as self absorbed and as vain as ever."

"Those actors playing Maureen and Benny can't keep their hands off each other," she added. "Something must be going on with those two."

Days later Idina and Tracie filmed "Take Me or Leave Me." In the powerful duet, the two women argue over their differences. At several advance screenings, the song consistently ranked as the best received number, even drawing applause.

"The only thing we miss in this performance is more of Idina singing," Christopher claimed on *Rent*'s DVD. "People love her voice. They want to hear more of her singing."

"Go see *Wicked*," Adam Pascal laughed.

Chris Columbus yelled cut for the final time on June 15. Once the director took a moment to breathe, he complimented his hugely talented cast, including the Broadway star.

"Idina Menzel is incredibly funny, charismatic, and has one of the strongest voices I've ever heard," he wrote on *RentBlog.com*. "She sparkles onscreen. She's unique and real."

Three months prior to *Rent*'s release, its soundtrack's first single "Seasons of Love" premiered. The signature theme debuted strongly on Billboard's Hot 100 singles at #68. When Warner Brothers Records released the motion picture's double

CD, it ranked #47 on the Billboard 200. The album also featured "Love Heals," an unheard Jonathan Larson composition.

*Rent* hosted its world premiere at Manhattan's Ziegfeld Theatre on November 17, 2005. Idina walked the red carpet wearing a stunning carmine gown. After the screening, she admired her friends' work.

"I was so taken with my own cast mates and their beautiful performances," she told *Playbill.* "Chris really captured something special about each of us. Anybody that loves the show will feel good about it, and people that haven't seen it

RENT: THE MOTION PICTURE
(Sony Pictures)

will totally fall in love with it. You sit in the seats, and the music comes blaring out at you, it's like an event."

*Rent* debuted on November 23, scoring 5.3 million dollars on opening day. The motion picture lost the top spot only to the blockbuster *Harry Potter and the Goblet of Fire.*

Unlike the stage production, though, *Rent* the movie received mixed reviews. Many complained that the show didn't capture its predecessor's excitement and heart. However, several critics praised Idina's standout portrayal.

"The musical highlights are Heredia's lively dance-and-drum bit "Today 4 U" and Menzel and Thoms' love-hate duet "Take Me or Leave Me." - *Salt Lake City Deseret News*

"Menzel is great, incredibly charismatic and fun." – *IGN*

"Casting most of *Rent*'s original Broadway stars is definitely a plus. Menzel, Rapp, Heredia, Diggs, Martin, and Pascal understand what it takes to make this story come alive and how to really belt out those songs." – *Hollywood.com*

At the year's end, *Rent* picked up several award nominations. The picture nabbed four nods at the Golden Satellite Awards, including Best Motion Picture and Best Supporting Actress for Rosario Dawson. Idina and company also picked up ensemble nominations from the Broadcast Film Critics Awards and the Washington DC Area Film Critics Association.

Perhaps *Rent* the movie didn't enjoy the breakout success like its stage incarnation, but the cast and crew took pride in knowing that it faithfully represented Jonathan Larson's vision. In the end, that's what ultimately mattered.

## "BENNY" & "MAUREEN" AT RENT'S PREMIERE
(Anthony G. Moore/PR Photos)

"I love being in a Disney movie.
I'm excited that my kids are going
to see it someday."

# EVER EVER AFTER
## Chapter Seven

In October of 2005, Idina starred in Michael John LaChiusa's *See What I Wanna See* at the Public Theater. The off-Broadway limited engagement co-starred Marc Kudisch, Mary Testa and Henry Stram. Based on three short stories by Ryunosuke Akutagawa, the show details several people offering their own versions of a murder.

Idina wanted to collaborate with Michael John for several years, so she pursued the role actively. Its off-Broadway status only made the project more appealing.

"There's less pressure, which allows for more creative process," she explained to *Playbill*. "We had time to try things and take risks. You don't have eight directors taking notes, giving you constructive criticism on the side."

Idina reinforced her reputation as a huge box office draw. Theatergoers flocked to see the star in a tiny setting. After the show opened, the musical added two weeks to its engagement.

The show earned stellar reviews. Michael John's nuanced score received many kudos, and the brilliant cast reaped high marks, too.

"Idina Menzel, who won (deservedly so) a Tony for playing the green-faced witch in *Wicked*, has a powerful voice and presence." – *Curtain Up*

## A FAN CREATION: ELPHAMAUREEN
*(Laura-Ashley Foster)*

"Ms. Menzel finds an aching authenticity, as well as original comic charm. She elicits shades of diffidence, sweetness and sourness sure to surprise those who know only her blockbuster vocalizing in *Wicked*." – *The New York Times*

When the musical ended its limited engagement, many high-profile talents courted Idina for their upcoming productions, including Andrew Lloyd Webber. The famed composer offered her the title role in *Evita*'s London revival. Ultimately, though, the actress turned down the role, unwilling to make a long-term commitment.

In September of 2006, Idina accepted a short run when she reprised Elphaba in *Wicked*'s UK premiere. Her presence helped the show break all West End records as British theater

ENCHANTED'S NANCY
*(Disney)*

A DISNEY PRINCESS
(Disney)

lovers snatched tickets. The actress also earned *WhatsOnStage. com*'s Theatregoers' Choice Awards for Best Actress in a Musical. She even met Prince Charles after the royal family member attended a special performance.

Idina loved London and considered it her favorite city besides New York. Yet she still missed Taye and her family dearly. At one point, Cara and her mother eased her homesickness when they flew over for a visit.

In feature film news, Idina landed a supporting role in Disney's *Enchanted* after director Kevin Lima caught her in *Wicked* and felt she'd be spectacular for a fashion designer role. The actress had never been offered a film without an audition and always dreamed of starring in a Disney movie. Yes! Yes, she would love to join *Enchanted*!

Featuring a score by Alan Menken and lyrics by Stephen Schwartz, *Enchanted* mixed live action and animation. The film follows Princess Giselle (Amy Adams), who after banished by an evil queen (Susan Sarandon) from her animated land, ends up in unpredictable, modern-day Manhattan. A divorce lawyer (Patrick Dempsey) and his adorable daughter (Rachel Covey) discover the woman and give her a temporary home. As she begins to fall for the new man in her life, who is engaged to a career woman named Nancy (Idina), her fairy tale prince (James Marsden) arrives to rescue her. Will Giselle return to her animated fairy tale, or will she remain in New York?

Funnily enough Idina's character was the only one which didn't sing. Amy, who began her career in musical theater, sang two major numbers, and *Hairspray*'s James Marsden also flexed his impressive talents. Even Patrick Dempsey sang a little bit.

The *Wicked* star, however, felt just fine about taking a break from singing.

"It was exciting to just be seen as an actress," she remarked proudly.

Although Nancy provided a roadblock for the romantic leads' imminent union, Idina ensured the character behaved kindly, avoiding a boring stereotype.

"I didn't want to portray her as the typical mean girlfriend," she stressed.

When Idina arrived on the set, she felt anxious about working with many prestigious personalities. Yet the movie stars viewed Idina as a celebrity, too. Sometimes Amy approached the singer sporting a mischievous twinkle in her eye.

"Can we sing songs from *Wicked?*" the Oscar nominee begged. "You play Elphaba and I'll be Glinda!"

Amy knew *Wicked*'s cast recording by heart and yearned to play Glinda in a film version. So Idina sometimes sang show tunes with *Enchanted*'s lead actress.

Idina also loved costar Susan Sarandon. She adored sitting near the screen legend and listening to her recount exciting Hollywood stories.

The most thrilling moment came during the filming of the picture's medieval ball scene. Idina dressed in a fancy princess dress and danced with James Marsden. To perfect the musical sequence, she and the actor took several waltzing lessons.

Idina and Taye attended *Enchanted*'s premiere at Hollywood's El Capitan Theatre. The beautiful actress wowed onlookers wearing a dark green Zac Posen dress. Later she partied all night with Carrie Underwood, Helen Mirren and even Mickey and Minnie Mouse. One could say that much like her character, Idina now lived a fairy tale life.

**ENCHANTED PREMIERE**
(Albert L. Ortega/PR Photos)

*"I Stand is about finding myself."*

# DREAMING A DREAM
## Chapter Eight

On January 29, 2008, Idina released her second full-length solo album entitled *I Stand*. The accomplished artist co-wrote nine of the album's ten songs and labored 18 months on the project.

Idina collaborated on *I Stand* with Glen Ballard, who produced Alanis Morissette's *Jagged Little Pill*. She and the musical powerhouse brainstormed by reading her diary entries. Sometimes they simply set up a microphone and improvised.

Each album's song stemmed from personal relationships. Idina penned "Where Do I Begin" as an apology to Taye after angering him. "Gorgeous" tells people to love whomever they want. In the personal "Rise Up (Cara's Song)," the songwriter urges her sister to pursue her dream of becoming a singer.

Because of *I Stand*'s relationships theme, Idina used the album's liner notes to acknowledge loved ones. She called Cara a hero, her parents an anchor and Taye her home.

On September 17, 2007, Idina premiered *I Stand*'s songs as Michael Buble's opening act at Madison Square Garden. When Warner Brothers released the album three months later, the singer celebrated by appearing on *The Today Show*. Later that day, she signed CDs at Times Square's Virgin Megastore. So many music fans, some sporting green makeup, turned out that the store issued wristbands to control the crowd.

**WALKING THE RED CARPET**
(Anthony G. Moore/PR Photos)

Music critics reacted positively to *I Stand's* songs and production values. Idina's songwriting and soulful voice consistently received lush compliments, too.

"[Idina's] singing without machines to "fix" her voice and without a ridiculous image to back her up." – *Pop Blend*

"You get a sense of who Idina is – someone who's loved and lost and who has gained power from that – and is obviously a very accomplished singer with a powerful voice." - *BBC*

"Her emotive voice is incredibly appealing, whether tackling blissful pop or heartfelt ballads." - *Boston Herald*

*I Stand* debuted at #58 on the Billboard 200, marking Idina's best selling solo debut. The album peaked at #54 in the UK. Shortly afterward Oscar winning singer/songwriter Melissa Etheridge emailed the singer to congratulate her. The superstar's daughter, a huge Idina fan, played the CD for her mother, who loved it.

Two hit singles emerged from *I Stand*. "Gorgeous" reached #3 on Billboard's Hot Dance Club Songs chart, and the ballad "Brave" hit #19 on the Adult Contemporary chart. The latter tune inspired a successful music video that featured Idina wearing an elegant wine-colored gown with flowing fabric that unwound as she walked about town.

Strangely enough, after spending the past few years on stage, Idina felt vulnerable singing as just herself. Suddenly she didn't have a character to hide behind.

"It's a little scarier. It's just me and my words and my stories," the singer told *Playbill*. "In that regard, it's more challenging, and sometimes more rewarding. People singing along to songs that you wrote, it's an incredible feeling."

Whatever happened, Idina felt fully satisfied with *I Stand*. She'd learned about herself as an artist and a person.

"I found an artist who uses her music, her voice and her speaking voice," she told *The Associated Press*. "I want to be known as someone who's authentic, true to the moment at any point in time and doesn't want to be pigeonholed."

Idina began *I Stand*'s tour in New Brunswick, New Jersey. Two backup singers, a drummer, bassist, guitarist and keyboardist comprised her band. Detroit, St. Paul, San Francisco and Los Angeles headlined the tour schedule. Chris Mann, a gifted vocalist who eventually found success on television's *The Voice*, entertained audiences as her opening act.

"To travel the country and perform my music is something I've always wanted," Idina gushed to the *Star Tribune*.

The recording artist even enjoyed her own tour bus. She and her band rode in the vehicle as they traveled state to state. Each person slept in their own cubbyhole, and they passed time by telling stories and watching DVDs.

In every show Idina displayed her trademark candor. The unpretentious performer always tickled audiences with her honest anecdotes.

"I try to be as authentic as I can and really be myself," she remarked. "I find comfort in connecting with an audience."

On May 12, 2008, Idina returned to the London stage, starring opposite Josh Groban and Adam Pascal in Royal Albert Hall's concert version of *Chess*. The musical chronicles the US-Soviet rivalry during the Cold War. American Freddie Trumper (Adam) battles Russian Anatoly Sergievsky (Josh) for the world chess championship. Chaos ensues when the Russian champion falls for Florence (Idina), the American's assistant. The show bombed on Broadway, but the endearing songs reached cult status among musical theater fans.

"The show didn't do particularly well," lyricist Tim Rice admitted to *The Deseret News*. "We changed it too much. A huge book was added in. But the music never went away... If I may be immodest, the songs were very good."

Theatergoers loved the concerts, which aired repeatedly on *PBS*. Reprise Records also released a popular cd and a hot-selling DVD.

Six months later Idina received a huge thrill when she sang for Barbra Streisand at the Kennedy Center Honors. The tense performer stood backstage waiting for her introduction. Was this truly happening? She flashed back to herself as a five year old singing "The Way We Were" with a thick Long Island accent. The memory made her smile. Yes, she was truly here, and she would give her idol a great show.

Wearing an elegant black velvet dress, Idina walked onto the stage and sang her heart out to "Don't Rain on My Parade." The smitten performer even changed a lyric by singing, "Hey there, Ms. Streisand, I am your biggest fan," directly to the legend. The moment brought rapturous applause from the audience, including President Barack Obama and honorees actor Morgan Freeman, singer George Jones, choreographer Twyla Tharp and The Who's Pete Townshend and Roger Daltrey. When Idina finished, Barbra blew her a kiss! Weeks later the floored performer also received a thank you note from her idol, which she placed on a shelf next to her Tony award.

"I think it was good," Idina later laughed about her performance. "I think it was heartfelt and in the moment and somewhat lucid."

In early 2009 Idina and Taye revealed that they were expecting their first child. Shortly before the actress' pregnancy reached the 30 week mark, her doctor's office performed an ultrasound to check the baby's progress.

"It's a boy," the technician announced.

Those three little words sent them into euphoria. A little boy! How fun! Plus their child would carry on the Diggs' family name. They had no idea, though, what their son's first name would be.

"We have a couple [names] in the running," Taye told *People Magazine*. "We'll see what he looks like."

On September 2, 2009, Taye was filming the ABC television drama *Private Practice* when a stage manager stopped production and pulled the actor aside.

"Your wife is in labor," he announced.

Several hours later, Idina, Taye and their family members took turns cradling their son, Walker Nathaniel Diggs. The new parents radiated happiness.

Parenting provided the couple the toughest, most fulfilling experience of their lives. One thing they didn't enjoy, though? Loss of sleep.

"When he takes a nap, we all take a nap," Idina told the *Star Tribune*.

Blessed with unbelievably talented parents, Walker displayed a natural musical aptitude. His parents frequently sang to him, inventing songs about teeth brushing or car seat safety. Forever performers, Mom and Dad regularly stopped mid-song to debate which notes best fit their improvised compositions.

Mostly their tiny son loved dancing. He created choreography to songs by Michael Jackson, Beyoncé and Bruno Mars. Walker also enjoyed singing the hits "Just the Way You Are" "All the Single Ladies" and "Rolling in the Deep."

Taye habitually rushed home just to watch Walker's latest performance. Though the doting parents took their son on fun outings, the family often just snuggled by the television.

"I just love coming home," Taye gushed to *Us Weekly*. "It's like a great prize waiting at home."

"I love his smile," he added. "He's always smiling."

Idina and Taye rarely relied on nannies, immersing themselves in Walker's daily activities and special occasions. On Halloween 2011, Walker dressed like a truck and Mom and Dad took him trick or treating around their neighborhood.

Idina also appreciated the quieter moments with her son. She loved holding Walker until he fell asleep. Sometimes she gazed at him incredulously. Had she really created such a beautiful boy?

"People say he mostly looks like Taye," Idina divulged to the *Pittsburgh Tribune-Review*. "He has his nose and the shape of my eyes. He's so yummy. My favorite thing is to feed him, rock him and put him down to sleep."

Idina never felt happier. She and Taye had been together for nearly 14 years. The couple had experienced rough patches, but they always cherished each other.

"The best thing about being married is having your best friend by your side constantly," she told *Good Housekeeping*. "Knowing that someone has your back."

While Idina was expecting Walker, she and Taye began watching television's smash hit *Glee*. Ryan Murphy's musical comedy about McKinley High School's underdog glee club displayed winning characters, snappy dialogue and a cast featuring numerous Broadway stars. The expectant parents watched the hit series weekly, remarking that they would like to be on the show someday.

Tony-nominee Matthew Morrison led *Glee*'s hapless misfits as Mr. Schuester, the affable singing coach who clashed with cheerleader instructor Sue Sylvester (Jane Lynch). *Spring Awakening*'s Lea Michele also starred as Rachel Berry, the glee club's overzealous, arrogant star. When the *FOX* show debuted, several reviewers noted the young singer's physical resemblance to Idina.

*AS SHELBY ON GLEE*
(FOX Broadcasting Company)

"*Glee* is a show for those of us with huge nerd love for musical theater (you can count yourself part of that group if you immediately notice the resemblance one main character has to *Rent* star Idina Menzel)." - *The Post Standard*

"Michele reminds me of a young Idina Menzel - in looks as well as voice." - *The Charleston Gazette*

*Glee* cast member Chris Colfer, who played Kurt Hummel, also noticed the similarity. The *Wicked* fan had even built a shrine to Stephen Schwartz's musical in his bedroom.

"I would love to have Idina on the show," he exclaimed.

In *Glee*'s first season, McKinley High covered *Wicked*'s breakout hit "Defying Gravity." Kristin Chenoweth also filmed a recurring role as failed Broadway actress April Rhodes. Given show runner Ryan Murphy's *Wicked* fondness, the show's fans created online pools predicting how long it would take the creator to write a role for the musical's leading lady. Perhaps she could play her doppelganger's distant relative?

After Walker's birth, Idina felt somewhat blue. The new mother adored her baby, but she felt anxious about the pregnancy weight she'd gained. As a result, she often prepared diet shakes, which Taye complained smelled badly!

One afternoon Idina's agent called with uplifting news.

"*Glee* wants you on their show," Bonnie announced.

"You're kidding?" the Broadway star squealed. "Taye will be so envious!"

Several weeks later, Idina received *Glee*'s script. When Walker took a nap, she settled down to read about her role.

It seemed immediately clear that her character Shelby, vocal coach of McKinley High's rival club, might also be Rachel's long-lost mother. The 38-year-old would play the fictional mother of the 26-year-old actress? Although her ego felt bruised, the performer quickly swallowed her pride.

"Glass half full," she told herself. "Glass half full. This is a great opportunity."

Once Idina arrived on *Glee*'s set, the age concern became a non-issue. She felt honored that the show's creator had written her an interesting, complex character.

"Ryan Murphy really, really appreciates Broadway talent," she gushed to the *Boston Herald*. "It feels good. When you're in Hollywood, it's all about movie stars, so it's nice to be appreciated if you have a theater background."

Motherhood had also mellowed the actress. Egotism no longer seemed important. The sleep-deprived mom skipped facials on filming day and learned her lines the previous night. Both decisions would have horrified her months earlier.

"I'm more in the moment," Idina claimed. "I'm less vain."

Viewers hoping the Broadway star would display her famous vocals weren't disappointed. Throughout Idina's lengthy storyline she sang everything from Lady Gaga's "Poker Face" to *Les Miserables'* "I Dreamed a Dream." When Shelby eventually left the show, *Glee* fans expressed dismay. Where had the popular character gone?

In actuality, Idina was preparing for a new tour. This time, though, the popular performer would sing with a symphony. She would also have the company of a sweet toddler.

*"I'm still the girl from Long Island that used to sing with a rock band."*

*FINALE*
*Chapter Nine*

In 2010 Idina teamed with Marvin Hamlisch for several symphony concerts. *A Chorus Line*'s composer won a Pulitzer Prize, three Oscars, four Emmys, four Grammys and a Tony Award. His famous works included "The Way We Were" "Nobody Does It Better" with Carole Bayer Sager and *Ice Castles*' "Through the Eyes of Love."

The blissful mom brought Walker on the road. She named her show *Barefoot at the Symphony*. A real life event inspired the quirky title.

"I like to perform barefoot, and I was choosing not to because I was with these symphonies," the revered artist told *The Washington Post*. "I thought I had to dress up more. One day I had no choice. I was traveling with my little boy. My back hurt from carrying the stroller and the car seat, and I thought there was no way I could perform in heels. So I threw them off and performed barefoot, and it was the best show I ever had."

Unlike her past tour's casual setting, Idina sang with the help of major symphonies. Long Island's very own played North America's finest concert venues, New York's Carnegie Hall, the Walt Disney Concert Hall in Los Angeles and Boston's Citi Performing Arts Center.

"It's a real milestone," she remarked happily.

"At first, I was tentative because I didn't want to lose intimacy that I can have with an audience," she told *NPR*. "A

## 2013 SAG AWARDS
(Andrew Evans/PR Photos)

vast group of musicians behind you could be overwhelming. But it's thrilling and I love it. I found a way that I can have the extravagance and also talk personally with the audience."

*Barefoot at the Symphony*'s song set boasted a wide range. Idina sang several popular works from her résumé. She performed three *Wicked* songs, "I'm Not That Girl," "For Good" and "Defying Gravity." *The Wild Party*, *Rent* and *Chess* also received representation, as did *Glee*. The New York native even sang two songs connected to her childhood, "The Way We Were" and "Tomorrow."

*Barefoot at the Symphony* earned the vocalist much acclaim. *The Denver Post* described Idina as the "Streisand of her generation." In fact, her concert series proved so popular that *PBS* taped the show when the tour hit the Royal Conservatory's Koerner Hall in Toronto, Canada. As an added bonus, Taye joined his wife for a charming duet and dance to "Where or When."

On August 6, 2012, Idina received devastating news. Following a short illness, Marvin passed away in Los Angeles. His death shocked the entertainment industry.

"My heart is broken," Idina told *The Charleston Gazette*. "[Marvin] made me feel so special. I love him so much."

"He taught me to be funny and spontaneous," she continued. "He made me believe in myself. For him to give me his time and mentor me meant everything."

Various legends attended Marvin's funeral, like Liza Minnelli, President Bill Clinton, Richard Gere and Diane Sawyer. At the touching memorial service, Idina sang *A Chorus Line*'s "At the Ballet" in honor of her dear friend.

Later that year, Idina won the lead in Walt Disney's 53rd full-length animated feature, *Frozen*. The family flick chronicles a kingdom trapped in eternal winter. A spunky optimist named Anna (Kristen Bell) teams with mountain man Kristoff (Jonathan Groff) on a journey to find her sister Elsa, the Snow Queen (Idina), and put an end to her icy spell. The mom felt proud to star in a film that her son would someday see.

"The movie is beautiful," Idina enthused. "I just recorded one of the songs. Kristen Bell and I sing a duet together."

On February 28, 2013, ecstatic producers announced that Idina would star in a new Broadway musical called *If/Then*. An original work, the show follows 39-year-old Elizabeth who moves to New York for a fresh start only to have her life affected by random occurrences and small decisions. The production would premiere on Broadway in spring of 2014.

Composer Tom Kitt and lyricist/book writer Brian Yorkey created the modern day work. The duo began *If/Then* shortly after their Pulitzer Prize winning musical *Next to Normal* opened on Broadway. Both men felt thrilled to work with the powerhouse vocalist.

"We couldn't ask for a more exciting leading lady than Idina Menzel, whose unbelievable talent, professionalism, humor and spirit have infused this character," they raved.

Idina felt excited to work with the new songwriters. However, the actress also felt comforted to reunite with *Rent* director Michael Greif and producer David Stone, who also presented *Wicked*.

"I've experienced the beauty of working on original musicals and was eager to find a project where the material was exciting and new and spoke to my heart," Idina gushed. "I'm thrilled to have finally found it - an original musical with a complex, flawed, and surprising central character that I cannot wait to bring to life onstage."

"I have loved collaborating with Tom Kitt and Brian Yorkey on the creation of this character," she continued. "And it is such a blessing to reunite with Michael Greif, who launched my career with *Rent*, and David Stone, who took good care of me with *Wicked*. I am extremely excited about *If/Then* and look forward to returning home to Broadway."

Broadway musicals. A hit television show. Rock gigs. Symphony concerts. Idina loved them all.

MACY*S DAY PARADE
*(Angela Giacalone)*

BAREFOOT AT THE SYMPHONY
(Ken Bergmann)

Still the actress couldn't be still. She constantly set new goals. Someday Idina hoped to take a stab at Shakespeare. She might even tackle a Tennessee Williams play, like her favorite *The Rose Tattoo.*

Whatever project happened next, Idina would embrace the opportunity with her monster talent, self-deprecating humor, hard work and professionalism. Not surprisingly, those traits had already earned her legions of loyal admirers.

"I love to write songs," Idina told *Directions Magazine.* "I love to put on makeup and play characters. I love to sing with rock bands and orchestras. I love to act in front of a camera. I love to do them all."

And her fans would always love watching her.

# ESSENTIAL LINKS

IdinaMenzel.com
www.idinamenzel.com

Idina's Official Facebook Page
www.facebook.com/idinamenzel

Idina's Official Twitter Account
www.twitter.com/idinamenzel

Idina's Official MySpace Account
www.myspace.com/idinamenzel

Idina's Official Tumblr Account
idinamenzel.tumblr.com

The Official Idina Menzel Youtube Channel
www.youtube.com/user/idinamenzel

Idina's Official Google+ Account
plus.google.com/+idinamenzel

Idina Menzel on Pinterest
www.pinterest.com/idinamenzel

*If/Then* Official Site
www.ifthenthemusical.com

*Wicked* Official Page
www.wickedthemusical.com

*Rent* Official Site
www.siteforrent.com

# DISCOGRAPHY

### Rent
Original Broadway Cast

### Still I Can't Be Still

### The Wild Party
Original Off-Broadway Cast

### Wicked
Original Broadway Cast

### Here

### Desperate Housewives
Music From & Inspired By

### Rent
Original Motion Picture Soundtrack

### Beowulf
Original Motion Picture Soundtrack

### See What I Wanna See
Original Off-Broadway Cast

### I Stand

### Chess
In Concert

### Glee: The Music
Volume 3 Showstoppers

### Idina Menzel

### Idina Menzel Live
Barefoot at the Symphony

## SUTTON FOSTER
### StageStars Volume 1

Musical theater fans first fell for **Sutton Foster** in her triumphant turn as the title character in *Thoroughly Modern Millie*. Since then the heralded triple threat performer has charmed Broadway audiences in a wide variety of memorable roles, playing a writer, a princess, a movie star, a nightclub singer and a Transylvania farm girl. Now the two-time Tony Award winner is conquering television as the lead in the critically acclaimed series Bunheads. A children's biography, *Sutton Foster: Broadway Sweetheart, TV Bunhead* details the role model's rise from a tiny ballerina to the toast of Broadway and Hollywood.

## ABOUT THE AUTHOR

**Christine Dzidrums** holds a bachelor's degree in Theater Arts from California State University, Fullerton. She previously wrote the biographies: *Sutton Foster: Broadway Sweetheart, TV Bunhead, Joannie Rochette: Canadian Ice Princess, Yuna Kim: Ice Queen, Shawn Johnson: Gymnastics' Golden Girl, Nastia Liukin: Ballerina of Gymnastics, Gabby Douglas: Golden Smile, Golden Triumph* and *The Fab Five: the 2012 U.S. Women's Gymnastics Team*. Her first novel, *Cutters Don't Cry*, won a 2010 Moonbeam Children's Book Award in the Young Adult Fiction category. She also wrote the tween book, *Fair Youth*, and the beginning reader books, *Timmy and the Baseball Birthday Party* and *Timmy Adopts a Girl Dog*. Christine also authored the picture book, *Princess Dessabelle Makes a Friend*. She recently competed her second novel, *Kaylee: The 'What If?' Game* and received a second Moonbeam Children's Book Award for her biography on Miss Douglas.

~~~~~~~~~

## BUILD YOUR GYMNSTARS™
### Collection Today!

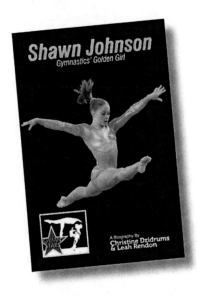

**Shawn Johnson**, the young woman from Des Moines, Iowa, captivated the world at the 2008 Beijing Olympics when she snagged a gold medal on the balance beam.

*Shawn Johnson: Gymnastics' Golden Girl*, the first volume in the **GymnStars** series, chronicles the life and career of one of sport's most beloved athletes.

Widely considered America's greatest gymnast ever, **Nastia Liukin** has inspired an entire generation with her brilliant technique, remarkable sportsmanship and unparalleled artistry.

A children's biography, *Nastia Liukin: Ballerina of Gymnastics* traces the Olympic all-around champion's ascent from gifted child prodigy to queen of her sport.

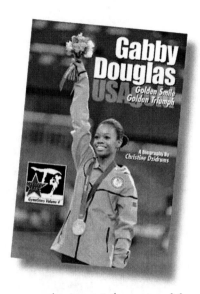

Meet the five gymnasts who will represent the United States at the 2012 London Olympics. *The Fab Five: Jordyn Wieber, Gabby Douglas and the U.S. Women's Gymnastics Team* tells each team member's life story as they rose from young gymnasts with big dreams to become international superstars of their sport. Discover the stories of **Jordyn Wieber**, **Gabby Douglas**, **McKayla Maroney**, **Aly Raisman** and **Kyla Ross** as they aim for gold in London!.

At just 14 years old, gymnast **Gabby Douglas** left behind her close-knit family in Virginia Beach, Virginia, to train under famed coach **Liang Chow**. The girl with the golden smile believed her sacrifice would someday lead her to Olympic gold.

A children's biography, *Gabby Douglas: Golden Smile, Golden Triumph* will grab readers as they experience the thrilling path the popular gymnast from the Fierce Five took on her way to becoming Olympic Champion.

**2010 Moonbeam Children's Book Award Winner!** In a series of raw journal entries written to her absentee father, a teenager chronicles her penchant for self-harm, a serious struggle with depression and an inability to vocally express her feelings.

"I play the 'What If?'" game all the time. It's a cruel, wicked game."

Meet free spirit Kaylee Matthews, the most popular girl in school. But when the teenager suffers a devastating loss, her sunny personality turns dark as she struggles with debilitating panic attacks and unresolved anger. Can Kaylee repair her broken spirit, or will she forever remain a changed person?

Meet **Princess Dessabelle**, a spoiled, lonely princess with a quick temper. When she orders a kind classmate to be her friend, she learns the true meaning of friendship.

# BUILD YOUR SKATESTARS™
## Collection Today!

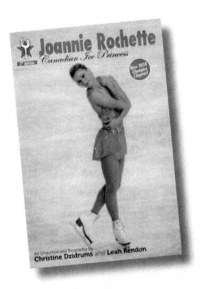

At the 2010 Vancouver Olympics, tragic circumstances thrust **Joannie Rochette** into the international spotlight when her mother died two days before the ladies short program. The world held their breath for the bereaved figure skater when she competed in her mom's memory. Joannie then captured hearts everywhere by courageously skating two moving programs to win the Olympic bronze medal.

*Joannie Rochette: Canadian Ice Princess* profiles the popular figure skater's moving journey.

Meet figure skating's biggest star: **Yuna Kim**. The Korean trailblazer produced two legendary performances at the 2010 Vancouver Olympic Games to win the gold medal in convincing fashion. *Yuna Kim: Ice Queen*, the second book in the **Skate Stars** series, uncovers the compelling story of how the beloved figure skater overcame poor training conditions, various injuries and numerous other obstacles to become world and Olympic champion.

**Jennie Finch** fell in love with baseball as a four-year-old when her mother started taking her to Dodger games. A year later, her parents signed her up for softball lessons and the young girl was instantly smitten. As a youngster, Jennie dominated travel softball and later became a star player at La Mirada High School in Southern California. During her time at University of Arizona, she set an NCAA record with 60 consecutive wins. Blessed with remarkable pitching ability, good looks and role-model sportsmanship, Jennie became a breakout celebrity at the 2004 Athens Olympics, where she captured gold with her team. *Jennie Finch: Softball Superstar* details the California native's journey as she rose from a shy youngster playing in a t-ball league to becoming softball's most famous face, a devoted mother of three and a legend in women's sports.

# BUILD YOUR TIMMY™
## Collection Today!

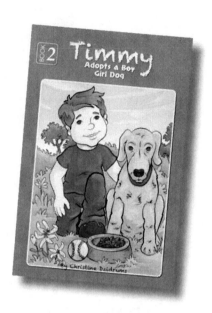

Meet 4½ year old Timmy Martin! He's the biggest baseball fan in the world.

Imagine Timmy's excitement when he gets invited to his cousin's birthday party. Only it's not just any old birthday party... It's a baseball birthday party!

*Timmy and the Baseball Birthday Party* is the first book in a series of stories featuring the world's most curious little boy!

Timmy Martin has always wanted a dog. Imagine his excitement when his mom and dad agree to let him adopt a pet from the animal shelter. Will Timmy find the perfect dog? And will his new pet know how to play baseball?

*Timmy Adopts A Girl Dog* is the second story in the series about the world's most curious 4½ year old.

Twelve-year-old Emylee Markette has felt invisible her entire life. Then one fateful afternoon, three beautiful sisters arrive in her sleepy New England town and instantly become the most popular girls at Forest Springs Middle School. To everyone's surprise, the Fay sisters befriend Emylee and welcome her into their close-knit circle. Before long, the shy loner finds herself running with the cool crowd, joining the track team and even becoming friends with her lifelong crush.

Through it all, though, Emylee's weighed down by nagging suspicions. Why were the Fay sisters so anxious to befriend her? How do they know some of her inner thoughts? What do they truly want from her?

When Emylee eventually discovers that her new friends are secretly fairies, she finds her life turned upside down yet again and must make some life-changing decisions.

*Fair Youth: Emylee of Forest Springs* marks the first volume in an exciting new book series.

CPSIA information can be obtained at www.ICGtesting.com
Printed in the USA
BVOW04s2132221214

380503BV00019B/641/P